BOA
EDITIONS LTD

Model Homes

Model Homes

Wayne Koestenbaum

AMERICAN POETS CONTINUUM SERIES, NO. 87

BOA Editions, Ltd.   Rochester, NY   2004

Second Printing, 2012

For information about permission to reuse any material from this book, please contact
The Permissions Company at www.permissionscompany.com or e-mail permdude@
eclipse.net.

Publications by BOA Editions, Ltd.—a not-for-profit corporation under section 501
(c) (3) of the United States Internal Revenue Code—are made possible with funds
from a variety of sources, including public funds from the New York State Council on
the Arts, a state agency; the Literature Program of the National Endowment for the
Arts; the County of Monroe, NY; the Lannan Foundation for support of the Lannan
Translations Selection Series; the Mary S. Mulligan Charitable Trust; the Rochester
Area Community Foundation; the Arts & Cultural Council for Greater Rochester;
the Steeple-Jack Fund; the Ames-Amzalak Memorial Trust in memory of Henry
Ames, Semon Amzalak and Dan Amzalak; and contributions from many individu-
als nationwide. See Colophon on page 96 for special individual acknowledgments.

Cover Design: Lisa Mauro
Cover Art: "House" (2002) by Jennifer Bartlett, courtesy of the artist
Interior Design and Composition: Richard Foerster
Manufacturing: United Graphics, Inc., Lithographers
BOA Logo: Mirko

Library of Congress Cataloging-in-Publication Data

Koestenbaum, Wayne.
    Model homes / Wayne Koestenbaum. — 1st ed.
        p. cm. — (American poets continuum series ; v. 87)
    ISBN 1-929918-56-9 (pbk. : alk. paper)
    I. Title. II. Series.

PS3561.O349M63 2004
811'.54—dc22

2004011599

BOA Editions, Ltd.
250 North Goodman Street, Suite 306
Rochester, NY 14607
www.boaeditions.org
A. Poulin, Jr., Founder (1938–1996)

 *for Steven Marchetti*

Model Homes

⊠ WARM-UP

1.

I lack a subject. (That's been said.) I need
    A heroine—not Mom, not Jackie O,
Not Anna M. Apostrophize my seed,
    Spilled building blocks eschewing embryo?
For many months I've foundered: Ash and Reed
    (My ruined novel), Andy, Liszt, *Tombeau*
De Couperin (Ravel), and now this half-
Baked movement, lurching iambs on the distaff

2.

Side—inchoate *chora*, Kristeva'd call
    My melancholic tendency to talk
Nonstop, to fill pink typing paper's hall
    Of mirrors with what garbagemen would balk
To claim from suburb curbs. I love when a ball
    Bounces below a cartoon's words, like Salk
Inventing cures and then rescinding them,
Fort-da assertions of a Tantric lingam.

3.

One shouldn't mix up poetry and essay
    Unless one likes being caught in a snafu
Aesthetic: rhyming diaries, prosa-
    ic. Capital offense! My errors queue:
A psychoanalytic poem's passé:
    Faux pas, to come off as a nervous Jew.
Dear reader, we are trained not to confuse
Art with analysis, or else we'll lose

4.

The meager literary capital
    We've saved. My longtime shrink's away this week—
And last—and the week before: the usual
    July vacation, which explains this sneak
Attempt to bolster sanity with real
    Pentameter's prosthesis, like the beak
Of a hummingbird I saw, this morning, enter
A daffodil's null, anhedonic center,

5.

Reprising last night's dream, when I held office
    Hours, at school, in the nude! I couldn't think
Where I'd misplaced my underpants. My sis
    Had quarreled with our Mom, and on the brink
Of fisticuffs, I told the rude Lutèce
    Sommelier that in my bathroom sink
(Lutèce now doubled as motel) I'd found
Red ants. Meanwhile my mother tried to sound

6.

Me out on whether chicken fricassee
    Might stop our family from going mad—
My brothers (two), my sister, me, and He
    Who Must Not Be Obeyed, my softie Dad
(Chauffeur, professor, doormat, refugee),
    Who shared my mother's *Île Flottante,* and paid.
"Paid" and "Dad": the two don't quite match up.
I found an earwig in my dish of ketchup.

7.

Awake, I watch that earwig reappear:
    Its double, dead, lies floating in my pot
Of lukewarm citron oolong tea. A seer
    Once told me, "You should think in twos: forgot-
ten magic will rain down if you can hear
    Systole and diastole of pregnant thought
Breathing, like lung-joined twins, *ensemble*—dream bug
And real bug, bound in Life and Art's bear hug."

1.

I nurse a deep distaste toward any form.
    Meter's the chain Joan Crawford ties her son
To bed at night with: what if chloroform
    Beneath his door makes deathly diapason
Of his confinement? Joan hopes he'll reform.
    (*Diapason:* octave.) Dropout nun,
Miss Andrews quashes fears with favorite things
In stereo. To discipline, she sings.

2.

Strict stanzas are a telephone: ring, ring,
    You guilty charlatan, leaving alone
Your family and friends—you ding-a-ling,
    Invective the P.E. coach, a Francophone
Spaniard, directed at the skinny gring-
    o boy I was, hiding a juicy bone
In my shorts, responsive to a thug named Joe
Whose chest hair told me mine might one day grow.

3.

The coach's calisthenics made me sick,
    And yet they gave him six-pack stomach slats,
Emblem of strength: beneath, perhaps a thick
    Sausage, as sleaze mags say. This dirty-brat's-
Quest for the pornographic epiphanic
    Unbricks my middle age's ziggurats.
Perhaps there's time to "cure" myself before
Old age turns me into a troll and bore.

4.

The coach's wife taught French. She told me not
    To wiggle in my seat. Though childhood
Enjoys repeated tics, a Gordian knot
    Maturity unties, her rigid Talmud
Exiled the wiggler, a skinny, femmy snot,
    To the corridor: when, punished, there I stood,
I saw a schoolgirl flee Biology:
A turd stained her white hose: shame's apogee.

5.

I dreamt that Susan Sontag criticized
    My writing—told me that I only cared
For fame and money. Cruelly she excised
    My tastes aesthetical, and then repaired
To Crete. While she was gone, I emphasized,
    In phantom lectures, her discreetly bared
Unconscious, where desires like mine made sport
Of daylit claims. While my astute retort

6.

Reduced her arguments to filigree,
    She came back from abroad, and asked me why
I'd bothered to rebut. As far as she
    Could judge, I was a literary fly,
Buzzing around a high festivity
    I couldn't join in human form, for I
Lacked clout, charisma, stamina, and grace.
And thus my idol mocked me to my face.

7.

Typical dream. Friends, strangers, have I lost
    Your trust? What can I say to earn it back?
Compare my sexual fires to Pentecost?
    Antically analyze my ego's "lack"?
Question my Dad about the Holocaust?
    (I'll strive to be my poem's father—crack
Its knuckles, wipe its bum, and tell it its
Right foot turns out.) Describe my mother's fits?

8.

When I try to sketch her daily hurricanes—
    Humor appears only in retrospect—
My brain and mouth shut down, I cede the reins
    Of proper speech, grow ornate, circumspect,
Surreal, sardonic—mining spider-veins
    Of irony in horror. I'd elect
To centrifuge the comic from the tragic
If I could master chemistry-lab magic.

9.

I step, a barefoot Cub Scout, on a nail:
    Doc's tetanus shot bores through my buttock's door.
(Knock, knock: reprieve: the plumber's here, with pail
    And wrench. My bathroom sink is clogged: a war
Between the water's urge to flow, and the veil—
    Muck, hair, grease, sperm—past which no force can pour.
If he succeeds in clearing it, I'll shave
Tonight and stop the drain anew.) Behave,

10.

Weak vacillating scribe! Stop playing dumb.
    Get back to Mom's "fits"—my first habitat.
I fear I overestimate the sum
    Of her belligerence. If her fits sat
Like angels on a pinhead, could they drum
    A minyan up? Maternal thermostat:
If I rehearse her heats, and how I felt
When household hell broke loose, my strength might melt.

11.

I don't believe in manliness, forswear
    Outdated virile protocols. It's best
To copy lady ways. But now, despair
    That I'm a rigid binarist, o'erdressed
Schematic wielder of *retardataire*
    Mythologies, takes root inside my breast,
Like Milton's snakes (or vultures) that return
To feast on carrion Mom, insulted bourne.

12.

Was motherhood a choice she could refuse?
    Four kids: she wanted more. I can't guess why.
We were too many. (Hardy.) Please excuse
    Me momentarily—these verses vie
With household chores—I'd rather not abuse
    The patient plumber, asking me to try
The sink to prove the mechanism runs.
Ecco! Its hole now opens, like a son's.

13.

I was to speak on radio at three
    O'clock this afternoon, but I got bumped
By a more important guest, leaving me free
    To write more mangled stanzas. If I'm stumped
I'll ride the subway to the Met and see
    The Chardin show, then catch the old guy trumped—
Nearly—by Alice Neel's life studies. Anon,
Massage at the Isosceles Salon:

14.

A bargain: forty-five for one long hour
    Of semi-consciousness, while a buff guy's
Hypnotic, unembarrassed fingers tour
    My colonies, whose expectations rise
Beneath the modest wrap. Paid paramour,
    He must see scores of guys who feign surprise
When, at the Swedish climax, "full release"
Occurs, unless the client's too obese.

15.

Masseurs, like the rest of us, are prejudiced.
    I, however, have a catholic
Libido, liking any shape of tryst.
    I'd happily massage an endomorphic
Wealthy gentleman. In fact, a tourist—
    Complected like a bingeing alcoholic—
Tried, on the train, to pick me up: my gums,
Just probed, were bleeding (watch the pendulum's

16.

Return to the poem's prelingual gory gist),
    So I, evasive, told the guy, "Next time."
I'll end this canto—not before I list
    The things I meant to say today (a crime,
To let erotic dreams unseat my ballast):
    I'd planned to sketch my mother's fear of grime,
Her furies, and the atmospheric dread
Shag-carpeting her *thump thump* warpath tread.

◈ Second Canto

1.

Today I worked out with my trainer, Lenna,
    Taut-bodied as my mother at the cold
War's height, the early '60s: Oz, Gehenna.
    Trade winds from nearby vineyards graced our wold—
Tract houses, cookie-cutter, with antenna,
    Fallout shelter, and agapanthus I've told
You about before, and won't reprise, lest I
Return to monomania's prose sty.

2.

Lenna makes me squat, lunge, press, lift, leap.
    We're trying to fix my back-and-neck alignment.
She called me "lean"! I hope our workouts reap
    A stronger frame—penultimate assignment
Before I go to my reward. Too deep
    For tears, my prophecy of time's adjournment:
The well-built Reaper stops me on the beach
To praise my biceps, and, black-gloved, to reach

3.

Into my underwear and store me fast
    Within his fingers, which transport us far
Beyond Fire Island, India, the last
    Frontiers of consciousness, to where a star
Beams in the nothingness, a friendly blast
    Of absence to assert I've crossed the bar
Beyond which no one living ever sees
Arousal. Sartre's smiling: he agrees.

4.

My father, squat phenomenologist
    Translating Husserl between the wars
(Korea, Viet Nam), ne'er raised a fist,
    And taught me that creators shirk house chores
By free will's force, diurnal facts mere grist
    For a mill that spins grief into Schubert scores.
Cooking the family's Sunday morning grits
Is not how one becomes a Horowitz:

5.

Great artists ditch distractions of the hearth.
    Stern teen with frizzy hair too wild for comb,
I wanted to become a hermit Barthes-
    Landowska fingering Pleyels, my home
A radon-filled phalanstery for the birth
    Of sublimating compositions, chrome
Amnesias, through which I'd lose the taint
Of human ties, and be Casals, bald saint

6.

Who knew, in San Juan, transports my piano
    Teacher explained—Busoni-transcribed Bach
"Phrase linings," her odd code catchphrase for volcano-
    Soldered marriages between two lock-
Jawed melodies that long to link in an O
    Of indissoluble caramel, like two Brach
Butterscotches sucked on in the car
Driving to model homes in rich Del Mar.

7.

Mom wanted any house but ours: we'd look,
    Sundays, at new developments, to see
If she'd be happier there, our block forsook.
    Across the street lived plump Mnemosyne,
"Block lady," gossip who turned her breakfast nook,
    Mornings, to a salon for Moms: burnt coffee,
Saltines, and cigarettes. Block ladies had
A credo: kids—small Judases—were bad.

8.

I wandered through their smoky, Wiccan grove
    And hoped propinquity might mollify
Maternal rage, revise it into love.
    Mnemosyne held yard sales: I dared not buy
Her clip-on earrings. Recent dream: Mom shrove
    My logorrheic sins, topmost this wry
Rehash of what should not be told. My butt
Muscles are sore from weightlifting. Rebut

9.

Body with mind, my father teaches: nude
    He rarely is—from vantage point of crib.
He flirts with waitresses, is never rude
    To hotel chambermaids. We snidely rib
His Venezuelan courtliness. I'm lewd
    In deed, word, wish, so ought to wear a bib
While writing: see the bile come pouring out
My mouth and land on *mère* and *père*, devout!

10.

I'll never have a kid. I'm far too selfish.
    Children kill creativity, I learned
At home. Unlawful, we ate pork and shellfish,
    Elbows on Formica, Mother's yearned-
For cleanliness a pipe dream: scrub each dish
    With Brillo pad, kid crud still clung. She burned
To write, and wore a housedress Gernreich-mod.
Beset, she wanted privacy. No rod

11.

Inflicted on our bottoms—no capital
    (I mean corporeal) punishment: just words.
And minor objects, destroyed, in just requital:
    A record, cracked; a poster, ripped. Can birds
Retract their song? Are kids' possessions vital—
    My torn-up Green-Chip stamp collection? Curds
Of cottage cheese (her lunch) in a Pyrex bowl:
Our kitchen was too cramped for her winged soul.

12.

Advice: don't bang the keys, but let the weight
    Sink to the bottom, naturally, and make
Kind sound. But how can I exonerate
    Unless I first narrate? It wasn't steak
She fed the sink's disposal, just cut-rate
    Ground chuck, the night her mood's Pompeian quake
Decided that a meal she didn't want
To cook because we'd crossed her Hellespont—

13.

Her borderline—would never come to pass,
    Would not make shapely hamburgers, would not
Feed kvetchy kids and abstract Dad. *Kick ass*
    Was her motto, metaphorically—high-wrought
Bright woman chained to housework with four sass-
    Prone children and a husband whom she thought
Distracted. Martyrdom was his main claim.
Like me, and like my father, she wanted fame.

14.

Still wants it—she's alive to read this. Yikes!
    Should I go on? Censor it later? Fill
In lurid details, so you'll see the tyke's
    Developmental stumbling blocks, and bill
The arch analysand? We rode our bikes
    On summer nights up Saratoga's hill,
Our wheels harmonious on Rhonda Drive
And Teresita Way. Names can't revive

15.

That time or make it seem like paradise—
    And yet my youthful woes were not the worst
In San Jose. Faye Dunaway in *Eyes*
    Of Laura Mars imagines crimes: she's cursed
With telepathic vision, a plot device.
    Don't be Christina Crawford, in a Hearst
Paper, exposing star-Mom's peccadillos.
I must remember that the root of *philos-*

16.

ophy—at least its prefix—is love, which works
  Genetically, through hormones, chromosomes:
I share her fitful, self-critiquing quirks,
  Her exiled voice, distrusting given homes.
She yells at Destiny, and Dad (who smirks),
  And kids, who grouse in private about poems
And ailments they'll wreak, soon, to pay her back.
To be a *mensch,* I'll choose another tack.

1.

My mother is a poet. Just like me.
    She started first, before I was born, then quit.
I confess I find our sameness slightly creepy,
    Though I'm a willing co-author of it—
Jocasta and her son's joint therapy.
    Typing these words, I need an amulet.
Ottava rima, be my chastity belt!
Protect my lips from incest's melting *gelt*!

2.

(It's Chanukah. I'm getting a sore throat.)
    I started writing poetry to place
My soul and fate in league with Mom's, demote
    Authorities, make my warped odes replace
Her past, redress her wrongs—my words a vote
    For her, my hand her deputy . . . A case
Of overzealous, crocked identification?
I took to heart her every imprecation.

3.

I'll sponge this subject till its drops are dry:
    My mother is a poet. So am I.
Thus when I write these words, I stare her "I"
    Straight in the eye, and her eye matches my
Jammed incapacity. Male vanity
    Is hardly relevant to poetry—
I'd write more powerfully if a cleft
Between my legs would form. I'd be bereft

4.

Without my stick (forgive the symbolic sphere),
　　But I'd not mind the surgery: a gift,
To metamorphose into Mom, to hear
　　Words in her Osterizer's whirr, to lift
Imagination up the ranch-house stair
　　To the second story, jerry-built, the rift
Between my parents widening while she wrote:
Her reborn lifework sunk their conjugal boat.

5.

That's her opinion. Their delayed divorce
　　Helped me escape the vise of California,
Warm and enmeshing as their intercourse
　　Before I was born, though I lacked cornea
To witness it. I'll shout until I'm hoarse
　　Regressive fantasies—aphonia
(The larynx lost) will keep me from being sued
For libel or for cocky attitude.

6.

I sweat when I write poetry: my pits
　　Are wet. I'm drinking frosty cappuccino.
My nose, not *retroussé*, is free of zits.
　　Flashback to '72, vacation, Reno:
Tired father, after motel bedtime, hits
　　My brother's butt. A day at the casino
Leads me to egg him on to say, "Hack-hack-
Qui-qui" (cute noise), which earns my Father's smack—

7.

Punishment unsevere, a pinkish rear.
    Though Pop was not, by rule, a spanker, once
He lightly whacked my head. (Mom said: "I fear
    Brain damage!") Memory: I'd press and bounce
My brow against his stocky frame, for Lear
    Was Dad, a hoary exile, with no ounce
Of policy. Mom's Lear, too: fickle, kind
To fools, storm-prone. Reason, return! Remind

8.

The poet that his task's to simulate
    Circuitous search for any primal scene
That, dipped into, might con, rejuvenate,
    Confuse—or make a dirty surface clean,
Maternal hygiene I repeat: she ate
    The scenery, her rage acetylene—
Plath's word, an apt one, to describe a fit
Perversely fun to watch and hear, to sit,

9.

Front row, applauding Mom's mad decibels.
    Her meltdowns—*unheimlich*—were process, due;
Consider it courtroom drama, when she yells
    About a messy backyard rockbed, a few
Stray bamboo leaves disturbing her: she tells
    The son, "Pick up each leaf, or I'll make you
Eat dirt." I stuff the leaves in a tin pail,
While, through patio screens, I hear her rail.

10.

I fear I'll quit tomorrow, before I've said
    The juicy parts: Mom's Bertha in the attic.
Problem: I never stop. The hour of lead
    Postpones the tale; the formal feeling's tick-
Tock chains my spirit to that dread rockbed.
    Okay. I knew a guy in fifth grade: Rick.
He, too, loved Cheryl. Cheryl loved me first,
Then switched to Rick. My ego's bell jar burst.

11.

Did I love Rick? He was my chlorine-blond
    Ideal, and so was Cheryl—the two of them
Well-matched, while I, slim, pale, small, odd, as I'm fond
    Of drumming in, disproved their tight theorem.
Ignored third wheel, I built my own *beau monde*
    By loving Rick, then Cheryl: this truth serum
I'm drinking (tea) speeds me to say that switching
Between two eidolons is more bewitching

12.

Than pledging troth to one: pursuing Rick,
    Then Cheryl, back to Rick, imagining
Rick watching me kiss Cheryl (is this sick?),
    Stage-managing a Rick-Wayne-Cheryl wedding,
Myself groom, bride, best man, priest, hierophantic . . .
    Erotic law: Rick is respite. Swearing
Fealty to Cheryl can be fatal. "You're *quit*,"
Her love-note said. She meant *cute*, but misspelled it.

13.

I loved submitting to my mother's rules:
    She taught me how to tie my jacket's hood,
To keep the bathroom sink drop-free—art's tools
    Analogous to household forms that could
Structure the mind . . . I want a pair of mules,
    Zebra. Note, I'm changing subjects: my blood
's a switcher's. I like to quit, and then return,
Contrite, to the spurned love, poulticing the burn.

14.

Max Grand's in town: my favorite prostitute.
    I haven't hired him yet, and nor has Steve,
Though we discuss him often. Max's cute.
    "No drugs, no attitude"—if you believe
His ad. I saw him on the train: en route
    To a john, or to the gym? We've a reprieve
From HIV—we're negative—and like
Monogamy, but sometimes urges strike,

15.

And what should boyfriends do? Negotiate?
    Max Grand is not a quandary I meant
To mention here—I'd hoped to sublimate—
    But meter's rockbed rules let me present
The unkempt gamut. Stanzas cannot hate
    Their author for transgressing: form's God-sent,
A striptease liberty. Max is expensive,
But cost is not why I am apprehensive.

▨ FOURTH CANTO

1.

I wasted twenty minutes on the Net
    Looking for bodyworkers, rent boys—Tantric
Services, like Suck-n-Surf, to whet
    My appetite, but the connection—click!—
Collapsed like an abandoned marionette;
    And when the link resumed, the only trick
I instant-messaged, Mark, refused to tame
My groin's disequilibrium—East's game

2.

Of forestalled climax, hardening to prolong
    Anticipation of release that comes,
If it comes, only after hours of wrong
    Turns, feints, deferrals, like the model homes
My mother coveted—could we belong
    To fine demesnes? Could we move far from Lum's,
Its hot-dog-diner television set
Broadcasting RFK felled by a bullet?

3.

I've lost the one ability I had—
    A knack for seeing divine coincidence
In arbitrary marriages, like Dad
    And Mom. A hard girl threw up at the dance,
High school, prompting a Vice-Dean's jeremiad:
    Her bad skin seemed a piece of evidence
In a legal brief defending my retreat
From sex, though I've become its exegete.

4.

What happens when I finish this disaster?
　　Perhaps we'll lie in Max Grand's rented arms.
Why do I try to write these stanzas faster
　　Than prudence warrants? Voodoo: meter harms
My birthright, strives, belatedly, to master
　　(Borrowing Bishop's rhymes) third-grade schoolmarms,
To make the reader drink iambic flow,
A suspect liquid, shaming, rococo.

5.

Today, who'll pop up on Rentboy-dot-com?
　　Rick M., Italian-Irish, masculine?
Or washboard-stomach eight-and-a-half-inch Tom?
　　Or Blair, a specialist in scat, toys, masks, and urine?
(Imagine how such roleplay strikes Blair's Mom.)
　　Or else I'll click on Asher, Levantine
Masseur, who does "out-calls" without a table,
Which means that bottoming's negotiable.

6.

Six years ago, I wrote a novel—*The Future*
　　Of Beauty, detective story also titled
Society for the Preservation of the Future
　　Of Beauty. Teacher, thinking himself entitled
To sex with students, after a misadventure
　　Kills the college president. Unbridled
Kiss-ass, I slept, thrice, with my teacher: she
Seduced me, half-unwilling pupil. We

7.

Performed the missionary. Should I skip
     The case's I-was-skinny-she-was-stout
And offer euphemisms? Should I rip
     Apart discretion's temple veil and shout
Details? Agog, erect, I watched her strip
     Her caftan off and suck my warm *umlaut*,
Though I was young enough to be her son.
No matter. I liked feeling overrun:

8.

"Magic! I screw a teacher and survive!
     She thinks I'm male, acknowledges my prick,
Considers it a dump truck worth a drive!"
     I wasn't a punk sans talent, but a Rick,
External guy, objectively alive,
     A piston or projectile jade-plant thick
With seed. I let it go. Her uterus
Had been removed: no eggs to bother us.

9.

Lust's provenance: forgoing intimacies,
     I want high-styled return to a lost dream
Of presence, moments when—at Safeway, Macy's,
     Pediatrician's—my mother's sharp words gleam
Prognosticating steel, like Edgar Cayce's
     ESP, or when, through sauna steam,
I scry a stranger's cock. My mother's "pussy,"
In my unconscious, is a wee bit fussy

10.

About drop-spattered sinks, or bamboo leaves
    In lava rocks, or messy bureau drawers,
Or desktop knickknacks not aligned, but heaves
    With love—or hypochondria—for her horrors,
We pests whose sinuses, on winter eves,
    Drip and congest, congest and drip, like oars
Beating the lake when Monty Clift lets Shelley
Winters drown. (She figured out he's nelly.)

11.

I'd love to drop this poem, and drop my pants,
    But literature's the solid artifact,
And sex a liquid superficial trance.
    (Banish dichotomies.) You'd think I lacked
Outlets! Take this unconsummated romance:
    Against the pool's stone edge I nearly cracked
My head, distracted by a swimmer: shiver
Crossing my spine revived the frost (*l'hiver*)

12.

Of boyhood discontent: nothing I write
    Can remedy the Faust-selfsworn-to-hell
Dissociation when a man looks right
    Through me, ignores—sideswipes—my asphodel,
Implying I'm not his type, and sends me light
    Years off from sense, so I become Ma Bell
In wartime trying to keep phone lines intact
While schools are shelled, and nurseries are sacked.

13.

My father holds me when I cry at night,
    A babe: repeated tale: when my tears stop,
He lifts me to the bedroom mirror's tight
    Recoil, and, seeing my eyes shut, then lets drop
The sleeper in his crib. That story might
    Prove naught. Now to the gym! With luck, I'll sop
Up voyeur thrills, freestyling through the pool—
To compensate me for this poem's hard school.

1.

I wonder if I've wrecked my lyric ear
    By years of workhorse prose. I'd love to write
Tight lines, with ample meat, but now I fear
    I populate the poem with slack and trite
Musings on bodyworker bubble rear.
    Useless. I'll read Apollinaire tonight
In bed beside my boyfriend Steve, whose book,
A Simenon, matchmakes Maigret with crook.

2.

Steve's cheekbones are Ghiberti doors, his nose
    (One day I'll write a blazon of his beauty)
Giotto-fine. He planted fairy rose
    Shrubs in our yard, beside the cherry tree.
He likes to clip my rhino nails, both toes
    And fingers. Ritual: to please me, he
Scrapes bubbles off his tongue with celluloid.
(Tongue's a topic he'd rather I avoid.)

3.

I hesitate to idealize the match—
    But I must make our marriage manifest.
We're mollusks, suctioned to the bed. Can't catch
    My bunny looking sordid when undressed—
Embracing me, he's balm against Nurse Ratch-
    ed flashbacks, rising at a bell's behest:
I hear the phone ring, and my Being stops—
Mom's voice—"Sponge dry the sink's leftover drops!"

4.

And now it's noon—lunch break. When I return
    I'll write another stanza praising Steve—
His biceps, neck, and jaw: no razor burn.
    Such Duccio eyes deserve recitative.
My finger climbs his forearm's Matterhorn
    Until it finds the lintel—no, the eave
Of his chin's roof . . . These complimentary
Conceits hide matters alimentary:

5.

I ate lasagna, vegetarian—
    The béchamel too salty—then killed time
Surfing for bodyworkers, and found Brian.
    In two hours I play Liszt for Pedja: I'm
Taking piano! My younger brother, Ian—
    I wanted to *bite* his babyhood. No crime.
Edible Ian was correctly reared
(The first time in my poems his name's appeared):

6.

We called him "Boob"—*Bub*—German slang for "boy";
    His soft stuffed animal, "Boob's Teddy Bear."
At birth, Boob had the Gutfeld nose, near-goy,
    And a cute red birthmark right where neck meets hair.
Within a year, it disappeared. Enjoy
    The infantile through retrospective snare:
A verse reverses first aversions: maybe
Meter permits me to digest the baby?

7.

In early photos, I look Moorish, lumpy,
    Carbon or coal seeming to shade my face—
A swart, Sephardic coating. I grew jumpy
    Around age four, when pale Miss Nancy's place,
On TV's *Romper Room*, gave way to humpy
    Jack LaLanne, of undetermined race.
Italian, like Steve? '60s: we drive
To downtown Oakland to see Nancy, live,

8.

Sign records, scarves, hats, books, at some toy store.
    We wait two hours. A star hates showing up.
Miss Nancy's face was my divine décor—
    Also, my first receptacle: her cup—
Her gaze—received my adulation's liquor,
    As she, broadcasted figment, let me sup
On her clear looking-glass's silver candy,
As Shirley Temple fed Warhola, Andy.

9.

It took me twenty minutes to write that stanza.
    Revising it will take me forty more.
Although they sound tossed off, like an "organza"
    (Warhol's code for "orgasm"), the gore
They spill is aria—Mario Lanza,
    Whose old LP I saw Steve's grandma store,
Unheard, in a sewing cabinet, till she
Bequeathed us household junk for reverie:

10.

Orange, her *Mario!* album hangs above
    My upright Petrof in the country, next
To Connie Francis, Doris Day (we love
    Her "Teacher's Pet"), and, looking oversexed,
Maria Callas, *spinto* hand in glove.
    (Vulcan, vanished, her voice still new-mints text.)
We've pinned the covers to our wall, tick-tack-
Toe checkers grid, pop queer found-art rickrack,

11.

Messy and casual as these lines, Scotch-taped.
    Perfectionists would use more lasting glue,
But I perversely value the misshaped
    Rough fever chart. A stumbling voice sounds true.
Steve's grandma—Nunni—died. I should have draped
    Mirrors. Now my charge is to imbue
My conduct with some portion of her charm,
To make *crespelle* and do Steve no harm.

12.

That's so oldfashioned! Almost Sara Teasdale:
    I found her in my mother's Oscar Williams
Anthology. Poems seemed a high-tech Braille:
    A way to beat incomprehension's doldrums,
Exotic as the ancient minor scale
    Or fruit we're not allowed to take past customs.
Evasive, I depend on simile:
Can figures of speech betray a family?

13.

My sister and I were, once, best friends. We played
    Barbies together: I provided Ken.
Her trump card: Francie. I wish we could have stayed
    Forever in our *Funny Girl* playpen,
Recycling *My Fair Lady* songs, old maid
    And bachelor, incest's empyrean.
Our Grasmere cottage period ended when
My mother caught my sister in the kitchen—

14.

Forbidden to use that room without permission—
    Defiantly making muffins—and their war—
Elektra meets Medea, open season—
    Turned me to ice, eavesdropping, behind a door.
I'd hardly renounce my roost as favored son
    To stick up for a sister growing more
Unruly by the day—though with good reason,
I see in retrospect. It may be treason

15.

To venture, at the risk of repetition,
    Into this mythic family dispute,
So I will end my tale with an excision:
    At Mom's request, my father did a root
Canal, unscrewing the knob from its position
    Guarding my sister's bedroom door—a mute
Hole in the wood, where once there twirled a knob,
Window through which I heard my sister sob.

16.

That breach—that open wound—that gaping beacon
    In the hallway's night (she'd barred the door, locked out
My parents, whose Yahweh-style retaliation
    Was ridding her door of its obscene pig snout)—
That port-hole, Cyclops, stole my animation.
    Frozen, I watched that relic of their rout,
And thought, *In eight days, I'll return to college.*
I'll write this down. I'll make it public knowledge.

17.

In college I wrote a story about the hole
    In my sister's door—prose too confessional,
Embarrassing, unclean, like the round mole
    On my left thigh—a birthmark vaginal
Or anal—Sing-Sing—penal: to fake parole,
    With shears I tried to cut it off, to annul
The bond. I wanted a pristine leg, sans spot,
Brown birth hole, mud dot, spilled internal rot.

▨ Sixth Canto

1.

I'm terrified: today the riff might end.
    I want it to continue until nine
Cantos beneath my belt serve to defend
    My soul against the fear a metric line
Kills spontaneity. It's fun to bend
    Thought to the form, as tablespoons of brine
Pickle the cuke—the cuke, in this case, being
Traumas the waking mind is good at fleeing.

2.

Trauma: an ugly word. It's time to get
    Dry laundry from the basement. First I'll swill
A health shake—ginger, orange, lime, and carrot.
    Goodbye, frail poem! I hope you won't get ill,
Abandoned in my old Selectric's garret,
    Shunned victim, incompleted as a still-
Born babe the doctors flush away. I've said,
In other poems: Mom's first child was born dead.

3.

Nine cantos and nine months aren't parallel
    And yet I often dream that I give birth.
Recurrently methinks a show-and-tell
    Critter, plant-cum-infant, anti-mirth,
Sleeps in my bedroom closet's crib. I, pell-
    Mell Mom, forget to water it. Its girth
Lessens: it wrinkles, browns: I find it dead
Next week—its feet the pillow for its head.

4.

What do I feel, seeing the rotten child-
    Plant desiccated from my negligence?
Relief. The problem: keep the cops unriled.
    In court, I do a fancy song-and-dance
Proving impunity, like Oscar Wilde,
    Or like a capo who thinks evidence
Of weakness is a fate to be avoided,
Triste as a toilet after tots have voided.

5.

As you can guess, I'm captive to that room,
    Foul sacred site of death and birth and sin.
In every private home, those cisterns loom—
    More than mere pits where we deposit urine.
Our bathroom doors had locks: child, I entomb
    Myself for every covert exploration—
And afterward, meticulously expunge
Clear evidence of pleasure with a sponge.

6.

Adult, I work at home—that way, I solve
    The bathroom question—keep my own, unique,
Unshared ceramic vessel to absolve
    Digestive system sins. To take a leak
Is metaphysically to dissolve
    First matters in a bowl, where solids speak.
I'll change the subject now: this is unpleasant.
I have a nickname for my waste: *a present.*

7.

I say to Steve, "I'm gonna give a present
    To the community!"—a code he knows.
I'll disappear for days, although I meant
    To make it quick. The gift my body sows
In the waiting furrow is a senate judgment,
    An act of *civitas,* kind as a Loews
Theater opening gratis to the mob.
Steve has his own code word for crap: *a job.*

8.

I'm starving now—I'll fry an egg for lunch,
    And place it on a bowl of jasmine rice—
But first, I'll cheat (it's ten o'clock)—and munch
    On chips, or else a lemon bundt cake slice
With Earl Grey tea to speed the tardy hunch
    Into a tidy shape. Perhaps an ice
Cream scoop—vanilla—in my coffee? Bless
The crisper for containing watercress.

9.

I'd love to write another stanza now
    But errands call: I've held aside a pair
Of glasses suitable for my high brow
    And pallor. (I've begun to lose my hair:
A beard might suit my rectilinear jaw?)
    These Alain Mikli frames are, oddly, square.
I usually opt for round. May I invoke
A childhood scene again? My glasses broke

10.

By falling out a ninth-floor hotel window
      In Mexico. Without their aid, the trip
Was blurry. Stomach nervousness: that pillow
      Of rice with *two* fried eggs (I pigged out), zip-
Coded presto down my gullet, caused, no
      Shock, cramps. Gorging, I bit my lower lip.
I need to pamper my digestive tract
If I hope to keep this gassy poem compact.

11.

Today, I lack a single sexual thought.
      I'm writing in a taxi, headed east.
Yes, I'm a dirty bourgeois pig. We're caught
      In traffic near the opera house. At least
I planned ahead, and, providential, brought
      (We just drove by the Café des Artistes!)
This tiny notebook, so a few clandestine
Jottings could describe my bunched intestine.

12.

Just now, I've ducked into a church across
      The street from the optician's—I couldn't wait
Till I got home to limn my stomach's chaos:
      I guess my greedy tendency to sate
Hunger too quickly, gobbling, equals loss
      Transformed to avarice. Family trait:
We don't put down our forks to sip our wine
Or chew before we grab more spit-grilled kine.

13.

Those lines—a wanderer's—were uncontrolled.
    (I took the subway home.) My stomach's calm.
I bought the Paris frames: a fashion threshold
    Crossed. Certainly perspicacious Mom
Could guess I loved Burt Reynolds's centerfold?
    She didn't force me to attend the prom.
(By chance, I heard the name "Steve Koestenbaum"
On the cabbie's radio. Mere *liebesträume*?)

14.

The problem was, she never liked my father?
    (Cf. "In Dreams Begin . . . ," by Delmore Schwartz.)
Or that my father never cared for her?
    Didn't the *Pathétique* and Linzer tortes
Unite them in *Weltschmerz*? Her biggest fear:
    Flying. And mine? Return of anal warts.
The doctor burned them off, at Hades' lid.
I'd like to think I was her cuddliest kid.

15.

I haven't had a hard-on for one hour.
    What's wrong? Perhaps the rain. Last night a guy
Caressed his crotch before me in the shower.
    I said, "So long!" A faithful gent am I.
Observe my new frigidity, my power
    To liquidate the lingam's glozing eye.
(Not cocks, but only sentences, can gloze.)
My mother went with me to buy new clothes,

16.

Before each new school year, at The Young Set,
    Swank Town-and-Country mall. She understood
Costume, as word-couturière Colette
    Discloses how a mother and her brood
Despise each other with a tourniquet
    Of love, chiastic napkin staunching blood.
Recall the Tampax smell in the bathroom pail!
We have two fruit trees, Steve and I, but hail,

17.

This year, battered our crop, so though a peach
    Or two feigned ripe completeness, when we bit
Into its flesh, we felt a deep rot reach
    Out from the pit and cicatrize the palate.
My mother made peach pies. She tried to teach
    How love and hate are hardly opposite:
Wishes cross wires. She feared we'd sicken, die.
And yet: in a kidless house, the sinks stay dry.

18.

That's too oblique. I'll eat some cold polenta.
    Her first child died when she gave birth to it.
(A baby boy, I think.) By the time my placenta
    Streamed outward, she could happily intuit
That I'd survived the womb's impedimenta.
    Ahead of me lay pleasures undergraduate:
Time to smoke pot, snort coke, meet Steve, and read
O'Hara—all the nerve I'll ever need.

19.

I can't end so assuredly: the truth
        Is tentative. My uncle had a kidney
Transplant: his daughter's present. (I'm uncouth
        To mention it.) Would my own parents bid me
To donate organs if theirs failed? Was youth
        A body part I gave—hip socket, knee?
Steve's wisdom teeth, tonight, will be removed.
I'll taxi the patient home—though Mother disapproved

20.

When younger brother last demanded rescue—
        A car ride to and from the hospital
For surgery. (He won: she drove.) In lieu
        Of filial piety, I dish out brittle,
Satiric portraiture. Perhaps she'll sue?
        Perhaps my nervous state's congenital?
Two lines is not enough space to describe
Predestined ailments that confine our tribe.

▧ Seventh Canto

1.

Well, here I am in Germantown, two days
    Maturer than the last time I checked in
To Hotel Poem. Alas, no laurel bays
    Festoon my brow. Where went divine direction?
Steve's making berry muffins. Kind, he stays
    Downstairs in our unrenovated kitchen
While I, upstairs, attempt to find fit words
For bovine thoughts that masticate in herds.

2.

I picked up Steve on Friday after he
    Experienced sedation and lost track
Of consciousness while Dr. Pedigree
    Plucked out two wisdom teeth. When Steve came back
From Valium's embrace, eyes sweetly bleary,
    A kindred faintness seized me—anorak-
Shielded from summer storm, in whey-faced panic,
Not mettlesome enough to tend the sick.

3.

My parents hired a nurse when our whole brood,
    Including them, fell ill. I'll count the ways
My mother loved me: mumps, flu, croup. Include
    Such sickbed treats as poached eggs, *Photoplays,*
Immunity from her uneven mood,
    Her gift for whirlwinds, vortices, mêlées—
Though aren't I spoiled and evil to request
In retrospect a mother like the rest?

4.

Downstairs, Steve's playing motets: holy tunes.
    I dreamt I babysat a silent cat.
It couldn't meow. Its gestures were dense runes.
    It licked, in parched dumbshow, my welcome mat:
News flash: it wanted milk! Five tablespoons
    Emerged from my flat chest's false automat.
I fed it rice cakes, but neglected to
Unwrap the plastic. Cat teeth tore straight through.

5.

My newest fear is that these lines are prose
    Instead of poetry, and that I'll be
Punished for not minding the gap. Prose grows,
    Like pregnancy, while sterile poetry
Tightens, reduces, crimps, corrects—and shows
    A contrapuntal breathlessness. Agree:
I've erred. Now, Steve is marinating steak.
To help peel Yukon Golds, I'll take a break.

6.

This morning: a massage without release.
    The guy does deep work, semi-sensual,
Skirting the client crotch. True, he's a tease,
    And yet I egg him on, to bend his rule
Against the illegit. His scentless grease
    Won't touch the goods. Perhaps he thinks me fool
For what my groin's engorged salutes convey?
While I deep-breathe and twitch, he acts blasé.

7.

My body vibrates, when he's done with me.
　　The joints convulse, as if I were in shock.
A pro, he doesn't call my wiggling freaky.
　　Just now I found a hole in my right sock.
When Steve discovers holes, theatrically
　　He rips the sock apart—a lesson, mock,
In how to master flawed accessories.
Should I stop telling you domestic stories?

8.

Update: I napped one hour with Steve. Rain stopped.
　　Drifting to sleep, I wrote more lines—dreamwork
Combined with diligence—but then I dropped
　　To Lethe. Though I planned for "Douglas Sirk"
To be the rhyme for "work," the meaning hopped
　　Rapidly elsewhere. Liszt conundrums lurk
In contemplated stanzas, but the sun's
Returned, outshining smudged *leggero* runs.

9.

Hell, I'll return to difficult Franz Liszt:
　　I'm practicing his "Dante" Fantasy.
The piece is persecuting my left wrist.
　　Con strepito, he indicates. My lazy
Pinkie neglects to call infernal mist—
　　Meat—from the low notes' bowels: it isn't easy
To be a romantic hero, to pound the keys,
To drink one's own dementia to the lees!

10.

I envy that precocious soloist
    Who played a Liszt concerto (number two)
With our youth symphony. I, trumpetist,
    From my brass section seat could clearly view
Her warhorse-worthy hands, which never missed
    Their marks, though I oft flubbed my entrance cue:
My trumpet fizzed and splat to underscore
Climactic pomp. Most brass parts are a bore.

11.

I learned two instruments. I always play
    Two instruments, so I can grandly quit
The more embattled avenue one day
    And then, when weary of its opposite,
Traipse back to the abased first stage and say
    Hello again to my rejected habit,
Ex-nun returned to visit the vocation
She'd given up for Herr Von Trapp's ovation.

12.

I gave up trumpet for piano, prose
    For poetry. Boys stole the stage from girls.
And now, I'm loving form again. One rose
    In our backyard has butterfrosting curls—
I can't attend to stanzas when my nose
    Recalls the rare aroma that unfurls
From its thorned volute. I gave up fiction. Why?
I like to abandon objects, hear them cry.

13.

Each joy or task I leave undone is one
    Less mouth to feed. Piano, you were such
A brat—too eager for my teat. Fiction,
    Your screams kept me awake: I couldn't touch
Your brow without disgust. No medicine
    Could make me love you, loud gauche trumpet, much:
I left you rotting by the curb. O West,
My natal California, mother's breast,

14.

I quit your shores, pretending to dismiss
    Your pink hegemony, your charms, your air
Or moist or dry, depending which I miss,
    Your San Francisco hills a fairy chair
In which my teenage body sits. The bliss
    Of not being there! State animal: the bear.
I left that beast behind. And now, back East,
Tenth Avenue, I pine for Wild West's feast.

15.

East, West: Mom, Dad: to give or to receive?
    The other principality, beyond
My grasp, beckons, and so, I self-bereave,
    Digress, detach myself from the near pond
In favor of a far resort. But Steve
    Remains. Meandering, I've never found
A port to rival his. He's grilling beets.
We must leave now, if we want decent seats

16.

At Rhinebeck's Upstate Films. Whatever's playing,
    Romance or comedy, Steve wants to go.
I'd rather stay at home, read *Faust*, obeying
    Only the persuasions of Mephisto—
But if I dither here, and write more straying
    Stanzas, then *faute de moi* we will forgo
Delights theatrical, and when we sleep
Tonight together, tumbling in a heap

17.

Of sheets—green/yellow flannel, infantile—
    I'll feel guilt flashes. I'm exaggerating,
But—truth—I fear these pointed lines defile
    Parents I've no business desecrating.
And while I'm listing errors: I've been vile
    To friends. I give them up the way a sing-
er abandons roles—the tessitura's wrong,
And so I rip my blood tie to the song.

EIGHTH CANTO

1.

Nights later, another film: Joan Crawford starred:
 A Woman's Face, directed by (gay) George
Cukor. Her character's face, at five, was scarred—
 Dad's flames. A plastic surgeon's scissors forge
A second face. Near-murderess, she's barred
 From pushing her young charge into a gorge
By the same plastic surgeon: riding by,
He catches Joan's infanticidal eye.

2.

I made Steve read Joan's bio; loving it,
 We plan to screen a retrospect of all
Her pix: *Trog, Rain, Berserk!, Chained, Straitjacket,*
 Possessed, Torch Song, Above Suspicion, Fatal
Confinement, Susan and God . . . The titles fit!
 Place names are sad, like the 1950s mall
Five minutes from my birthplace—Valley Fair,
Where Mother bought me Carter's underwear.

3.

An apple gave me fortitude to write
 Those lines, and now I need a berry muffin.
Blood sugar deficit? My appetite
 Precedes the clock: too early now for tiffin.
I'd love to waste my life with tongue pressed tight
 Against a drowsy organ—next of kin—
Foot, nipple, elbow, penis—it hardly counts
Which zone or sex, as long as my mouth mounts

4.

The object at a snug degree to find
    Moist hibernation that will help wheeled time
Reverse, the cogs unmesh, the aging mind
    Regain its fontanelle's soft paradigm.
Last night, while I played Liszt, my big behind
    Sweated pathetically, in pantomime
Of the waterfall where Joan in *A Woman's Face*
Sends to his death her lover and accomplice.

5.

She posed as babysitter for the kid—
    Governess, as they say in MGM—
But underneath propriety she hid
    Hatred of Mary Astor's diadem,
And child stars whose fate is undecided—
    Will Jackie Coogan grow up butch or femme?
I shouldn't waste so many lines on Joan—
A reader's trust is only mine on loan—

6.

And yet I tire, dilating just on *madre.*
    The psyche seeks a stellar substitute,
Like Joan, to cancel pathos. It's okay
    To trumpet old vendettas if I mute
The horn, lest its invasive roundelay—
    Stone-deafening recital—hurt my root
Of being, Mom, who has a grief-prone heart,
Who bore four children, giving up her art,

7.

At least until I was in high school—then
    She recommenced, and, afternoons, would lock
The house's door so she could write sans children
    Shattering concentration. Three o'clock:
She'd let us in. Twin, I took up the pen
    The year two friends—girl, boy—first touched my cock.
My mother wrote—and, also, stopped—at Radcliffe:
Her stymied genius made my organs stiff.

8.

I don't mean "prick": I mean my guts, the stuff
    Internal—stomach, colon, lungs. She rode
Our house like Einstein harnessing the rough
    Bronco of relativity. Our abode,
As she perceived it, clenched her with its handcuff.
    Dad, too, felt trapped, believing that he owed
Nothing to any god but his free will.
Too bad his kids were brats, his wife, a pill.

9.

When she reads this, will there be nasty fallout?
    Will she perceive the buried, mournful praise?
Were I a parent, I'd give me "time out,"
    Newfangled punishment: Kid disobeys,
He's exiled to a measured, bordered bout
    Of silence. Last night's dream: teacher, I raise
Hell in a normal school by skipping class—
Remedial—and then I kiss the ass

10.

Of post-romanticism's greatest poet:
    I tell him I've been reading Tennyson
And Coleridge. White lies. He feeds me suet,
    Soft spoonfuls, and I long to be his son,
To boff his throbbing baccalaureate,
    To analyze *Critique of Pure Reason*
In bed beside him. Reader, here I go
Again: I long to be Dad's alter ego.

11.

Can you bear to hear the genealogy
    Of *Model Homes*? I was reading Kenneth Koch,
Who practices a pop ecology—
    Recycling looniness, like Andy's Coke
Bottles, in forms without psychology,
    Hygienic processes—sitz bath, foot soak
(As when I had persistent plantar warts)—
Following Koch, I figured that the arts

12.

Of randomness and chance improvisation,
    Which I have practiced under Schuyler's wing
(Imaginary—we never met), need fusion,
    Given my limitations, with the Swing
Of comic meter: reports on my queer union,
    My bathroom fears, my parents bickering,
All packed in Brillo boxes only Byron
Could fabricate. I'm not his chosen son.

13.

Too fond of popularity, I write
    For magazines like *Vogue, Allure,* and *Spin.*
What kind of poet am I? And now, look, light
    Verse! (I'll counterfeit my own assassin:
That line seems awkward as an overbite
    Destroying an up-and-coming starlet's grin.)
No more bourgeois collusion! *Vissi d'arte.*
I'm reading Crane. I've joined the aesthete's party.

14.

The birthday meal I asked for and received
    When I was young: Kraft Macaroni & Cheese,
Cube steak, white cake. Thus treats were interleaved
    With trauma. Let us hope confession frees
This writer to craft civil, post-bereaved,
    Respectable routines—poems built to please,
Not merely to unstop his hair-clogged drains.
Butchers imprinted squares on cube steak: pain's

15.

Insignia. I'd strategize my bite
    To coincide with the meat's crisscrossing edge.
Kraft noodles, stirred, made swamp sounds that invite
    Comparison with coitus. One groin's ledge
Suctions the mate's and whispers "slurp." Insight
    Is auditory. Wading in the sedge
Of section's end, I hear my own conception,
When Mother felt the gush from Dad's erection.

16.

And now I'm off to lunch: a *crêpe complète*—
    Reward for finishing another canto—
Gruyère and ham, and egg that's barely set.
    Can't wait to feel my molars waltzing *lento*
Into the melt. Like *Faust* at the old Met,
    My devil teeth persuade the yolk to go
Limp, and succumb. My heart breaks for the egg.
I also pity the ham. It has to beg

17.

The crêpe to bind it to the egg in warm
    Embrace. If only sentences were not
Such labyrinths! Returning, I'll reform
    The rhymes, pepper the poem's ass with shot,
Put it to bed, and hope that when the storm
    Of my revision's rage has passed, the tot
Will be alive. Time now to eat my crêpe.
It's in poor taste to use, as figure, "rape,"

18.

Which does not—by the strictest standards—rhyme
    With "crêpe" . . . For lunch, I wandered to The Big
Cup, not Gamin, and had a lousy time
    Guy-watching. Natch, I gobbled like a pig,
And now the undigested tries to climb
    Down the blocked chute (not to be infra dig).
To ease the flow, a closing metaphor:
My mother's moods pricked holes in my gut's shut door.

◈ NINTH CANTO

1.

I turned down, kids, an opportunity
    To sit near Debbie Harry in the flesh!
Who's she? A punk rock star, whose unity
    Of features I see magically enmesh
Deneuve's, Moreau's, Bardot's, and Vitti's beauty.
    In Empire Diner, her pet dog on a leash
Outside, Ms. Harry, with a friend, lunched. I
Did not revise my route, but *walked on by,*

2.

In the pop song's words, and, stoic, headed here,
    Gamin, for my foreshadowed *crêpe complète.*
It's Wednesday. Anxious time has passed, my dear
    Semblable, and I've promised to beget
More lax, marauding lines. Last night, my rear,
    The seat of every dread, was drenched in sweat
As I lay sleepless, planning stanzas. Now
I'm off, once more, to get my gums probed. Ow!

3.

But first I'll linger here to narrate dreams:
    No longer young, I fly to San Jose,
My natal zone: its kiddie park, clean, seems
    A dirty movie theater where I play
The fairy beldame's coachman-rat who screams
    "Why have I changed?"—aghast at transforma-
tion to a quasi-human chaperone
For Cinderella, who can't drive alone.

4.

He must obey: the rodent has a crush.
    Not merely dream: in real life, I played rat
On Junior Theater's stage, while, home, toothbrush
    In hand, I listened to Mom's raging scat,
Bebop, and tried to second-guess its ambush.
    Playing provocateur, not diplomat,
With cluttered closet, messy sink, and sass
I pushed my tense materfamilias.

5.

Back from the periodontist, who prescribed
    Rinses to kill my gum bacteria.
Floss rituals he carefully described.
    A tissue probe is no Illyria,
And yet I love the tightly circumscribed
    Patient-and-doctor bond. Diphtheria,
Mom's caution vanquished you. Her Dr. Watson—
Mine, too—saw four kids doff her full womb's Stetson.

6.

A birthing womb is only like a hat
    To someone sheltered—me—who's never seen
That organ in its agon. Nor like a bat,
    Baseball, is mankind's phallus. Nor argentine
Are coital pleasures. What am I getting at?
    The body's simple. Best not to demean
My mother, or myself, with simile—
Like Dionysus, son of Semele:

7.

In my first book, a prose account of men
    Writing together to pretend they were
A woman giving birth, I tried to fashion
    Fictions for my desire to be at war
With anatomical predestination,
    To make a vulva out of my back door.
A Freudian case, my version of the birds
And bees replaces fetuses with turds.

8.

I sent an escort e-mail praise last night:
    "You've got a hot ass, Dan!" I've not heard back.
Did I compose my horny mash note right?
    His silence wounds me, as when shivers rack
My spine while I am sulking on a flight
    To Tokyo. A girl I long to hijack,
Clara, is paying court to other guys.
Doubtless you think that I am telling lies—

9.

I've changed the loved one's name, but really, she
    And I were traveling to Tokyo
In 1975—Youth Symphony
    Goodwill ambassadors. She played vio-
la. (Keeping words—despite rhyme's tyranny—
    Intact, I could have said she played oboe.
In fact, she moonlighted on tympani.)
Moping, I hoped she'd see my agony

10.

And rescue me. At first she seemed flirt-proof,
    And yet that trip would culminate in us
Bathing together—inaugural, aloof,
    Untactile chance to show my virgin penis
To a pubescent girl. Not yet a "poof,"
    I was, nathless, no Israelite Adonis.
She called my body "nice," but flattery
Could not recharge libido's battery.

11.

I saw her chest, but failed to fathom *breast*
    As straight synecdoche for *lust*; I saw
Her pubic hair, which seemed like lemon zest
    Stirred into batter with whole milk and raw
Egg yolks to make a cake that's not the best
    Dessert you've ever tasted, though your maw
Is glad enough to tongue it while you wait
For sweets that taste a little less like skate.

12.

High school: I wrote three pages of a tale
    About this venture into nudity.
My story ended, "Clara, am I male?"
    I summoned her spirit during dread P.E.
And prayed that loving Clara tipped the scale
    Away from scopophilic crudités—
Asparagus spear and carrot, flashed in gym.
In aioli I dipped the witnessed limb.

13.

I've probably said too much about a girl
    Who seems a flimsy symbol—hetero hype.
Years earlier, I loved a cultured pearl
    On a tiepin's mount. Beau Brummell guttersnipe,
I'd craved this birthday gift: I'd seen it curl
    In its Penney's box as the philosophic pipe
Conformed to my maternal Grandpa's mouth
When Brooklyn came to monitor our growth.

14.

He wasn't pleased. A strict man, stricter than
    His *fille*, he was a word-besotted tyrant—
More fussy than tyrannic—and no fan
    Of San Jose. Rhetorically he'd rant
About faith's absence from our spick-and-span
    Hebrewless house, blithely unobservant.
He sang "Tit Willow," but he disapproved
Of the effete, unmanly way I grooved,

15.

Bell-bottomed, on my toy menagerie.
    If I deported all my teddy bears,
He said, in calculated bribery,
    He'd buy me anything. I hid the dears
Beneath my bed—dust-bunny sanctuary.
    Believing my ruse, he drove the rental car
To Discount Records, sealing the catamite's
Capitulation with *Mikado* Highlights.

16.

Will you permit the poet an iced tea?
    I need some strength, internally applied—
For in my stomach now disport the free-
    Radical traces of the times I tried
To toe the line and failed: authority
    Retaliated: in my gut the pied
Intractables persist, like my mute stuffed bear . . .
Forget Darjeeling. Break out the Sancerre!

17.

Not yet. I'm in an early wound's environ . . .
    Despite quotas, and a taste for deli,
My mother's father wrote a dissertation
    On Grecian aspects in the works of Shelley
And Keats—plus, if I'm not mistaken, Byron;
    Anglophile Grandpa coped with vermicelli
On the *QE2*. He wasn't a bad sort,
Though proud, inordinately, of the wart—

18.

He called it by the gracious name of "wen"—
    On his cheek: its gravitas, protuberance
I feared, demands descriptive acumen
    I sorely lack. This poem's my Salome dance,
But where's my Herod? Chicken's in the oven.
    Steve's at the gym. I'm plotting rash romance—
Squeezed-in appointment with a "cut" masseur.
Paid rubs, like rhymes, anesthetize, not cure.

◼ Tenth Canto

1.

My French bread's rising in an unwatched stove.
    Hot tea cools in the freezer. Water's here,
Desk-side. I've never felt a keener love
    For "boobies," Steve's, than last night—ecosphere
Incomparably cozy. Mazel Tov,
    Poet, pursuing plaudits for your Greer
Garson routine! Yet why am I ashamed
To mention joy? Must "lyric" equal "maimed"?

2.

I read Thom Gunn and Paul Muldoon last night:
    Intimidating precedents. I can't
Compete. Steve's reading *Joan of Arc.* A kite
    Gnaws at my gut. (Taste dictates fewer slant
Approaches to the plot: drift's impolite.)
    Afraid to be a milquetoast sycophant,
I irritate my friends and family,
Who leave me gumming this forced homily.

3.

Tea's cold enough to ice. I'm drinking it.
    Will I decide to burn this flabby hymn
When it is done? My father lived in Summit,
    New Jersey, several years—interim
Address among a gravityless surfeit
    Of houses. Peter's wandering museum
Had branches in L.A., Detroit, and Plano.
Before he took up Plato, he played piano.

4.

Attempting Mozart now—I'm putting Liszt
    Aside for a week, which makes me feel adrift
From strength—I note, sham musicologist,
    How the sonata-allegro form can sift
Repressed incomprehensibles, like tryst
    (I dreamt that Mother, reading me, was miffed)
And trauma—mixing tesserae to make
A normative, tiered sweet, a wedding cake.

5.

My mother telephoned. I picked it up,
    Expecting Boris, the piano tuner.
The Petrof's paranoia needs a checkup.
    (Avoid surrealism's trap. I'd sooner
Incinerate the poem than hear it hiccup
    Colicky fake-Rimbaud non sequitur.)
My heartbeat races when my mother speaks—
Orgasm interrupted as it peaks.

6.

Steve called: he's coming home in half an hour.
    Mock-courtesan, I'll primp for bacchanal,
Shaving, taking a fifteen-minute shower.
    He knows my housework skills are minimal.
I leave the kitchen counter full of flour;
    My vacuuming is adequate, not anal.
Today he wears his new red-orange striped shirt.
No perspiration mars it yet, nor dirt.

7.

I put my poem aside to critique *Faust*—
    Jarrell's translation, back in print. To write
A book review, I had to give up ghost
    Designs I'm wandering through, a dizzy knight
Errant unequal to Byronic joust.
    Now I've returned from prose, and in despite
Of odds, I'll push this monster up the hill—
If only its wimple soared, like Miss Bertrille!

8.

Remember Sally Field's *The Flying Nun?*
    Hip nuns, a popular motif: *The Sound
Of Music*, "Dominique." Naive homespun
    Pornography: after my parents found
The nasty photo that I took, girl's un-
    derwear, sixth grade (I, kneeling on the ground,
She, on a stool, short skirt no obstacle
To lens), there rose a local debacle:

9.

Her Dad drove by to claim the negative.
    My mother, though, was secretly amused:
She never thought "pervert" pejorative:
    The felonies which left her psyche bruised
Were floutings of her fixed imperative
    To wipe the sink dry after it was used.
Recurrent dream: the toilet overflows:
The carpet, wall-to-wall, absorbs the Po's

10.

Excess, to such explosiveness inured.
        Now Steve is home—with Camembert. Goodbye.
. . . I'm back—with tidings. After lunch I toured
        The yard, and saw a bunny. I stood by
And watched it nibble grass, its Being cured
        By nutrients beyond the naked eye.
Watching, I froze, not wanting to disturb
Its greedy feasting on our bitter herb.

11.

Flies—gnats?—revolved around my gazing brow,
        And when I raised my hand to brush them off,
The bunny sensed my movement (broken vow
        Of faithfulness?) and hopped away, to quaff
In other yards. I failed my friend somehow—
        Wiggling, I shattered the suspended trough
Where bunny nursed. I nearly gag on rabbit:
Though eating vegetarian's not my habit,

12.

In Rome I won't go near *coniglio*,
        In Paris, far from *lapin* I remain.
A bunny, like a baby, has a "popo"—
        Our childhood synonym for "butt." Like "Wayne,"
"Popo"—the word—is always apropos.
        When Mother said "popo," she sounded sane—
Wise guardian of my safe-deposit wealth,
The hole I only navigate with stealth.

13.

I dreamt of a crumpled fifty-dollar bill—
 The perfumed greenback, petaled, like a rose,
Curled out the spendthrift ATM with a will
 Of its own, and no receipt. And yet I chose
To do my business at this crazy till!
 My stamp-collector friend stood by me—close
Enough to kiss—but we were only ten.
Our pubic funds were meager, and *verboten*.

14.

Commuting hour's arrived. From downstairs, Steve
 Advises, "Traffic might be bad." In prose
It would be difficult to say I cleave
 To him as tightly as the garden hose
He's wrapped around the plants so they won't grieve
 When we are gone but will receive their dose,
Daily, of automatic water. Boxwood,
Poppy, and lavender concur: Steve's good.

⊠ Eleventh Canto

1.

Today I have a horrible stiff neck.
    It seems symbolic. Of derelict
Poetics? Sloppy weightlifting? Low-tech
    Loquaciousness? Prosaic lines erect
With childhood memories—flashbacks, priapic,
    To Dad, who—falsely?—thought himself henpecked?
Steve went to Boston for a funeral—
His best friend's father. Maybe it's immoral

2.

To mention death yet leave the lost one nameless:
    David Troy, of Natick, for the record:
Word-loving history teacher. I must confess
    To feeling guilty. No poor orphaned ward
Of the state, I've living parents to oppress
    With lines they can't respect, a poem too hard
On decent folks who gave me music, books,
Melancholy, and, if not good looks,

3.

At least strong teeth. Our gums, I've said, are poor,
    But not our bones. My cautious mother drank
Milk when we wintered in her womb obscure,
    And listened to sonatas while she sank
To naptime slumber. Fine pre-natal care
    From Dr. Watson: though he's dead, I thank
His ghost for handling Mother's panicked call,
Prescribing Dimetap, poor-man's cure-all.

4.

A tablespoon of Dimetap or Dim-
	etane (the second vowel's sounded: Dime-
Ah-Tane), a sticky syrup, busting crime,
	Poured from an autumn-purple jar, bedtime,
Cut through each mucus clot and rogue enzyme,
	And spread a Mom-munificent mild clime
Down from the palate to the stomach's core:
When I was feverish, she would ignore

5.

My bellicosity and borrow surgeon
	Manners, concerned that my environment
Be calm. Next door to us lived a curmudgeon
	Whose daughter had burned thighs: an accident,
He said: spilled coffee. Daily I'd serve sturgeon,
	Whitefish, and lox, but Steve demurs. (I meant
To push the poem away from hospital
And morgue, and back to our *élan vital*.)

6.

My stomach's sore. I overate: crêpe, tea,
	The usual. My Gamin waitress smiles
When I, poseur, show up, notebook in tow.
	"Tow" doesn't rhyme with "tea." Oops. Cute kid, Giles,
Our neighbor, five, yells out his bedroom window,
	"Dad, don't touch my penis!" Natch, this riles
The father, doing nothing of the kind.
We all have synonyms for front and hind

7.

Quarters: a little boy we know said, "Mommy"—
    (A girl I loved in college)—"where's my *b*agina?"
Bagina never was a sight to thaw me,
    Though I respect it. Mother to *Regina*
Turned one hundred today: like a Commie,
    Or dead Diana, I smash the royal china.
Consider me a slapdash chambermaid
To squeeze Queen Mom into a form both staid

8.

And idol-shattering. Ottava rima
    's Brit, or Byron was, until he left:
Incestuous bond, *furtiva lagrima,*
    Club foot, word-craft's inverted woof-and-weft.
Remove the circus makeup with Noxzema,
    Poet, and keep your tone intact, not cleft
Between a Pagliaccio and a Puck
Dying to give King Oberon a suck,

9.

Unless Titania objects: Queen's mad,
    She wants to sodomize the sprite herself.
My dream-cast Bottom is, I guess, my Dad:
    I'm Ghibelline to his *pax*-seeking Guelph—
A get-go Zionist, displaced nomad.
    Bedtime: I kiss each toy upon my shelf
Good night—adieu, as well, to sheets and floor:
If I ignore a fay, it might grow sore

10.

As my prick tip that fateful day the soap
　　Enjambs its sting into the opening.
"Mommy, my pee-pee-thing's on fire!" I grope
　　The *petit chose*, young miser reckoning
His real estate, his rising stocks, his Hope
　　Diamond ring. I should be polishing
That line instead of telling you Mom's shower
Was no man's land, barbed wire, except that hour

11.

On Sunday nights, when I was old enough,
　　And could transcend the bathroom with the tub—
The kid's retreat—and be a Romanov,
　　Sultan of the maternal, dripless hub,
The master bathroom, with its shower, fluf-
　　fy rug, and plugged-in toothbrush, which I'd rub,
In teenage years, against my royal pole:
Hubris. No Pasha, my penis was pure prole,

12.

And, commoner, it had no visiting right
　　In Mother's chamber, where the auburn kit,
A zipped-up vinyl purse, kept out of sight
　　In the top left bathroom drawer, stored items fit
Only for her, though on good days I might
　　Be granted access to the leathery mitt,
Which held nail scissors, file, and not much else.
And yet it seemed to register her pulse—

13.

For when I summoned chutzpah, and unzipped
    The kit in privacy—I often took
That liberty—my mind's jump-roper skipped
    Backward to prior wordlessness, sans book,
Sans syntax. Hyper-verbal Mom equipped
    My ego's quiver (though her aim mistook
Its target), kindergarten's first day, saying
To Mrs. Crandall, teacher (I was playing

14.

Along already, thrilled to be advanced),
    "Wayne's a reader." Wrong. I'd merely paged
Uncomprehendingly through books, and chanced
    To translate pictures. Soon, brother-upstaged
Short wiggling third-grade perv, by sex entranced,
    Hoarder of *Playboy* pinups, underaged,
I read adult fare. Essays on "the nude"
Came clothed in words, so words became my rood.

15.

At recess, in third grade, by jealousy
    Or pique inspired, a kid came up to ask
If I could read the fine-print argosy
    I held, *Britannica*'s Volume M, a cask
For "Motion Pictures"; I intoned the entry,
    At least a paragraph, mechanical task,
To flaunt precocious carnal literacy.
The lad might have been making fun of me;

16.

He might have been impressed to see a shrimp
    Reciting, in high-pitched voice, such handsome words.
This poem is recess, and, preposterous imp,
    Unlikable, I'm Siegfried pulling swords
From stone encyclopedias, a limp-
    Wrist heldentenor braving Bayreuth's boards,
In shoes that barely fit, with a lead weight
On my back, that makes me stoop, and hesitate:

17.

Have I yet mentioned that I used to stutter?
    Until third grade. A fat-faced classmate mocked
My stumbling proclivity: I'd utter
    The same syllable twice, to see it locked,
Laocoön, in one serpent shudder
    Of sense. All words were difficult, and blocked
Delivery of the sentence. Even *egg*.
My mother taught me how to spell. My leg—

18.

Forgive the repetition—bears a birthmark
    Precisely like the one on her left ankle.
Or right? I'd know that rivet in the dark.
    The twinned stains join our convict bodies, rankle,
And prove our bond: sign of the matriarch.
    Where did Dad's stigmata hide? "Sanka'll
Wreck his health," I feared. "Must fathers eat
Herring and marzipan?" It's time to meet

19.

My trainer (how indulgent!), who helps me shape
　　A frame distinct from Gregor's—Kafka's insect,
Wet-dreaming drudge. Upon return, I'll drape
　　More stories over rhymes not quite correct.
Perhaps I'll Patty-Hearst the poem—mind-rape
　　Its messy lines. I made—thus should protect—
The critter. But I'd like to see it dead.
Too much is streaming through its cluttered head.

❖ Twelfth Canto

1.

Are these words tantamount to matricide?
    Such questions jinx a poem already frail,
In need of endless speed—the will to ride
    Headlong beyond time's categoric jail
Into a blue so boundariless I've tried
    To subdivide its grail, to no avail.
Echoes erupt to mimic doubled pleasure,
Presence, simultaneity—in measure.

2.

Let this one be the cloudy canto—vague
    And purposeless, entirely abstract,
Without the usual body parts or *blague*
    Or pretense that neurotics must not act
Sublime. I, too, would like to be a sage,
    To flee the timebound cell of daily fact.
Writing this meditation violates
My sanctum, and the trespassed zone pulsates,

3.

Blinks on and off like a tooth removed, the gum's
    Vibrations trying to nurse the unexpressed
Back into speech—sore hole in the mouth for crumbs,
    Bacteria, and spit to build their nest.
Critics will say that my scant plot succumbs
    To potpourri, that I'm too self-obsessed.
Indeed, piled high upon my bed are clothes
Fresh from the wash: see, here the language grows

4.

Pedestrian—apartment life, my chores . . .
   I'm drinking coffee, iced. At five I play
Mozart for Pedja. Zoom to trauma: sores
   On medical-textbook pricks—VD's moiré—
Taught me, in public library corridors,
   What happens to our organs if we flay
Them daily with our hands or with the warm
Receptive mouths of "trade" in uniform.

5.

I tried to space each rhythm-method session:
   I didn't want to probe my groin's archives
Repeatedly, lest I use up my ration
   Of spunk. Did self-abuse give me those hives
That spread across my stomach, post-emission?
   Our Dr. Watson, from whom health derives,
Prescribed a cream to minimize the swelling.
Thermometers were touchstones of our dwelling:

6.

Inside the mouth, the gauge's silver nub
   Poked at the jointure between tongue and teeth,
Provoking fear that I might lose my stub—
   Speech-granting organ—severed from beneath
By the unmanning wand. Deer ate the grub
   Steve planted—daffodils—so should we wreathe
Our field with toxins to keep beasts away?
I don't want my wild bunnies poisoned: they

7.

Are not my enemies. Nor was that rod
    My mother stuck inside to measure heat—
Running a fever, I became a god.
    She must have stuffed that stick into my seat,
Where she'd have felt the infant hole, tightwad,
    Refuse her entrance. Birth of an aesthete:
How can I know what Mom and Pop seek there,
In that pink spot not yet ringed round with hair?

8.

At breakfast, beside Concentrate and pill,
    Red One-A-Day, and orange juice, Mom sat,
Depressed, zoned-out, staring, without will,
    At lemons painted on a rattan mat,
Daub purchased in Carmel. Remote, immobile,
    Eyes coldly narrowed, she refused to chat.
Signal: a mouth cloaked with a nerve-stiff hand.
By fit possessed, she threw her wedding band

9.

In the kitchen trash. The ring survived just fine:
    Did Dad retrieve it? Her thermometer—
Was it not also his, paternal sign
    Of labile, potent mercury? "Peter!
He's running a fever!": much could she divine
    From 99 degrees. Those millimeter
Insertions in the infant ass present
No pain if Vaseline procures consent.

10.

I'm sure that she—or he—slopped on the grease
    Richly to moisten the compliant rear
As in the days of pederastic Greece,
    When penetration was an atmosphere,
A purple influence—crème de cassis
    Clouding white wine. We overrate the clear.
And yet I fail at Lisztian nimbus, never
Persuading lightning-flash to sound like fever—

11.

While Mozart I can make—though amateur
    I am and will remain—sound nerveless, cool,
Don Giovanni turned to gracious neuter,
    A gelded politesse, passion on schedule.
Curving my fingertips, I trade God's grandeur
    For grass blade, teacup, thimble—minuscule
Ecstatics—and turn my back on unities
Of time and place that bring wit to its knees.

12.

By forty-three, my voice should have matured,
    Attained meridian. Soon I'll assault
Leftover pasta: smothered onions secured
    To noodle strands by butter, Vouvray, salt,
And Parmesan. The half-sweet wine's endured
    Since '88. I can't afford Meursault,
But Muscadet and Touraine from the Loire
Taste pure, and stretch the vinous dollar far.

13.

Loire! The river's name, like a shofar,
    Or Galli-Gurci's "pretty mockingbird,"
Resounds with tidings—not things as they are
    But as I wish they were, a ball gown shirred
And ruched, a Duchesse de Guermantes, a star . . .
    I lean on *Loire*, my last book's final word,
Because my shrink is gone—whom I once told,
"Analysis might steal my poem's Rhine gold"

14.

(Not that I've much): I feared that poetry,
    A source that loves to vanish, would escape
If she discovered my secreted country,
    A drifting mind, words altering landscape
Without explanatory corsetry
    Or dress-hooks keeping surfaces shipshape.
Metaphors make my inner regions mine.
I'm writing now against a strict deadline:

15.

It's past lunchtime, and soon I must conclude
    Today's endeavor. May I take a break
For nourishment? Don't think the poet rude:
    He's calling recess for the reader's sake.
—Returned, depressed. I'm in a wretched mood.
    Notice, I'm imitating Mom: mistake
And detail trouble us, but the big picture
Goes kerplonk. We care about the fixture

16.

But not about the light. Now watch me fuss
    About the poem's periphery, and miss
Its troubled core. Steve shouts out, "Lucky cuss!"—
    A phrase from *South Pacific*, which we lis-
ten to while driving home to London Terrace
    Apartment complex, where I broadcast this
Public service announcement: I have no talent.
I'm fake, like Henry James's Verena Tarrant,

17.

A girl, by Olive Chancellor o'ertaken,
    Pretending to be a raving medium.
As poet, I'm a prisoner, forsaken
    Infant left in Byron's stadium
For bulls to eat, though I had undertaken
    To cure their omnivore delirium.
My books of prose are falling out of print.
Sufficient reason, I suppose, to sprint

18.

Through stanzas, trying to speed the publication
    Of this rough-scanned and rudderless conceit.
I wish my words were met with jubilation
    Instead of skeptic jeers. (A poem's defeat,
Some purists justly say, is self-description.)
    Our breakfast history: cream of wheat
In the '80s; now, Steve makes us oatmeal.
If only verses were mere cereal,

19.

Moist pulpy grains that I could, toothless, suck.
    I might go to the pool before my lesson:
I'll see my virile friend, with any luck,
    And he may kindly forward me a vision
Of furred, redemptive meat. See, when I'm stuck
    In a flawed line, discontent with indirection,
All I need to do is find a man
To stare at: like the magic tryptophan,

20.

A substance, found in cheese, that brings on sleep,
    A nude man, if he's built the way I like,
Slows down to safer speed my manic jeep.
    Too bad I echo dated Wilhelm Reich,
Who tried to cure neurosis with a leap
    To climax, slow insight replaced by shriek
And sob. (I'm oversimplifying.) Dad
Is not a Reichian, but, faddish, had

21.

An Esalen phase—and though he skipped massage,
    His hippie colleagues, Mr. and Mrs. Gray,
Gave hands-on lessons in the mountains. Sage,
    My father taught death workshops, nights, to pay
For costly children. Underneath this page
    Lies my indebtedness to him, the lay
Preacher, and to my poet mother, who speak
Through medium me, as if my crude lines leak

22.

Seminal or menstrual fluids from their minds
    Derived. (Out, damn inversion!) For the speech
I give at high school graduation, a grind's
    Tribute, my mother helps: she wisely reach-
es in a recent *APR* and finds
    A Louis Simpson protest poem (impeach-
ment, Nixon's, is my *idée fixe*) to sew
Into my sermon: Father says I owe

23.

My existential bent, flashed in the speech,
    To him. (My sharpest thoughts are secondhand.)
I try to read between his lines, to beseech
    His book (*Vitality of Death*), "Who planned
Our household randomness? Don't leave me, Teach,
    Stuck in this free-will nothingness of San
Jose, without belief in a kind force
That rules our actions, and permits remorse!"

24.

The high school speech coach says to memorize
    My earnest valediction, to impress
The public, but I choose to fix my eyes,
    Passive, on that much-underscored address,
Borrowed from parents who are just my size:
    Five feet, five inches—six, with chunky dress
Shoe heels. Why treat my folks as if their huge
Bulk looms, needing stanzaic subterfuge?

25.

My father's mother, Ilse, was much shorter.
　　'40: she dies: widower Ernst bans Mozart
From the mourning house, then weds Carlotta Bayer,
　　His boss's ex. Long story. A doctor's art
Today could save poor Ilse, manufacture
　　A sound prosthesis for her failing heart.
My father doesn't talk about his past,
Although he mentioned early typhus, the last

26.

Supper we had together: he'd lost half
　　His body weight, he said, and almost died.
Caracas: his parents' graves lack epitaph.
　　Unvisitable marble stones now hide
Beneath more recent dead. Their autograph,
　　A signature outwitting genocide,
Imprints this poem, despite its filial scorn.
Had Ilse not been dead when I was born

27.

I might not have been born: no tragedy:
　　My father might have stayed put in Caracas:
I never would have suffered accidie:
　　I never would have rued my mother's ruckus,
Or caught her gift for gallows comedy:
　　I never would have bedded down with Bacchus.
Mom sits in a bathrobe, eating Concentrate,
1970, and I can't mitigate

28.

Her sadness. Staring at nothing, she's confined
    To the nothingness of our unjust demands,
Our deadening selfishness. My double bind:
    Her mood's the force that drives these typing hands.
Why can't I let her be? I've half a mind
    To end this poem and telephone Max Grand.
My lift-off tape's run out. I can't erase
These words, nor raise them from the commonplace.

❖ THIRTEENTH CANTO

1.

I've switched from Liszt and Mozart to a prelude
By late Romantic Sergei Rachmaninoff—
Hardly a soporific interlude.
Tonight, my father comes to town. Don't scoff
At me, reader, for wanting to conclude
This stanza with Fania Marinoff,
Carl Van Vechten's wife, mayhap his "beard,"
As these lines beard the strange way I was reared.

2.

My father e-mailed me to say he's lost
My number. Wonder what his slip-up means.
I'm slow today. Hung over. Robert Frost
Said form was like a net. I'd eat Peek Freans
For lunch as stand-ins for the holy Host
If I thought crisps could dissipate the screens
Dividing me from what I want to say.
Rachmaninoff commands; I can't obey.

3.

His music's difficult: too many notes.
I want this canto's flow to match the Rhine,
But I'm distracted by the vague dust motes
That populate the air above this line
I'm typing now. I wish Joyce Carol Oates
Would telephone to say this mess of mine
Excites her: then I could go on. Each name
I drop's a clue: my chemistry craves fame.

4.

The shock a name gives is olfactory—
    A toilet spritzing Jicky as it flushes.
Names are my infidel phylactery:
    The tale of Moses in the bulrushes
Is stored within the leather treasury
    As, in star names, reside my infant crushes.
I dreamt last night that Julie Andrews starred
In a *Poppins* remake: the blurry camera, barred

5.

From sharpness, could not spy the wear and tear
    Of age, and left me timeless, pacified
By what will never change, or what can't bear
    Clear focus's cruel scrutiny. I lied:
It wasn't *Poppins* redux, but *State Fair*
    Transformed into her private *Iliad*.
A paid informant, mole, and talent scout,
I didn't boo, but clapped when she came out

6.

To give a live-performance *Odyssey*
    Mimetic as the Mississippi River.
Face-lift? To speculate is heresy.
    Time spared the face but sacrificed the liver?
(Libelous dream! Thus I, snide Pharisee,
    Knock down my idols.) Slowly she moved, a Tiber
Winding toward the fountain in the mall
Where Mom took me to Macy's every fall.

7.

These stanzas take an Alpine concentration.
    I'd rather lie down on the floor and sleep,
As when, a child, my stomach craved purgation—
    And so, post-meals, I'd curl into a heap
Of overalls and V-neck, animation
    Ceasing, and when the ache died down, I'd leap
Again to action, nonstop worrier
Whose gut, like Hermes, played mind's courier.

8.

My stomach carried messages, as wombs
    Hold fetuses and then deliver them.
This biologic paradigm assumes
    The soul conforms to Galileo's theorem.
Spinoza's? Nietzsche's? Some such father looms
    Above my crib like an all-seeing golem;
No wonder I'd prefer to flee from form
Into depression's cozy college dorm.

9.

Despair's our alma mater. We graduate
    Each year, and then are hurled back to the start;
We take the tests again, and perorate
    In composition books, and when that art
Is mastered, faculties expectorate
    Our bodies back to the birthing room, apart
From closure: there, we huddle, unborn spawn,
Waiting once more to feel our first breath drawn.

10.

How can I tell if this is doggerel?
    Is there a god to judge these matters, ask
Tough questions, smack the meter? Shall I spell
    The moral out for you? Above each task
Presides my mother's maiden name, Orgel.
    She donned her father's strict schoolmaster mask
And helped me write my college application:
She typed it, fussing over hyphenation.

11.

I'm goofing off—playing hooky from the scene
    That ruled the dozen cantos previous.
Block lady, I'll flash back to you: Noreen,
    Across the street from my youth's devious
Address. Behind our kitchen window screen
    I cursed, then ducked. My aim was obvious:
I'd screamed, "Fuck you, Noreen!" Did Noreen hear,
Or guess the source, a buck in his tenth year?

12.

My neck's still stiff. Be safe. Avoid the gym.
    Be abstinent: no random naked men.
(Prudence would indicate a pseudonym.)
    Perhaps I'll change my free-weight regimen,
Which strains the neck. Don't squat, curl, bench-press, swim,
    Or exercise the unridged abdomen.
Do nothing that will move the neck! (Craning
To see a guy undress is also straining.)

13.

Form's vascular: its limits keep me hard.
    I shouldn't use such metacritical
Vocabulary while I'm playing bard.
    Meter's a tongue depressor: medical.
Dr. Watson, dead now, was our lifeguard:
    In dreams he cuts my cord umbilical
Again and again, and gives the shots that knock
The bearer out (forgive me) like livestock.

14.

Female anesthesia was the fashion.
    After one Watson visit, Mom bought me
(My ears and throat ached, and my face was ashen)
    The Bible—based on the Ava Gardner movie:
Nude pix of Adam and Eve! The widescreen version
    Stopped, I think, at Moses's Red Sea
Or Noah's flood. The pelvis-gripping scenes
Occur before our Maker intervenes,

15.

Creating shame: I'd fixed my sights on Eden,
    The naked years, before Eve's hair grew long
Enough to cloak the zone beloved by men—
    Some men, not me. Memory may be wrong:
Adam was played by an Italian
    Resembling my Steve? To end this song
Domestically suggests that God was right
To lock up paradise that wasteful night

16.

He found shy Adam tying on a leaf
    To cloak his newly prurient *choucroute*.
Seamed-nylon-stocking-wearing Mrs. Leaf,
    My first grade teacher, gave us Juicy Fruit,
When school began, as teasing aperitif,
    But henceforth forbade gum, as gray, hirsute
Yahweh proscribed the fruit he'd pointed out
As Eden's best—surpassing sauerkraut.

17.

I stole a mini-gospels from Books, Inc.,
    Because the text was tiny as a locket.
That night, my mother, by the laundry sink,
    Questioned the thief, in whose tight trouser pocket
She'd found the pilfered, holy bobolink.
    "I paid for it!" I perjured, on Mom's docket.
She told Dad, "Telephone the store." What then?
We'll keep intact that cryptic fable's hymen—

18.

Because I have a date with Steve at Bright
    Food Shop in seven minutes. (Time's not fake.
It's fact.) Must run to lunch! Our schedule's tight.
    He'll order berry flapjacks; I, crab cake.
He'll offer me a Jonah's-whale-sized bite.
    My vulpine stomach, afterward, will ache.
The moral's clear: my paradise is Steve.
To meet him in five minutes, I must leave.

◼ ABOUT THE AUTHOR

Wayne Koestenbaum is the author of three previous books of poetry: *Ode to Anna Moffo and Other Poems, Rhapsodies of a Repeat Offender,* and *The Milk of Inquiry.* He has published one novel, *Moira Orfei in Aigues-Mortes,* as well as five books of nonfiction prose: *Double Talk: The Erotics of Male Literary Collaboration; The Queen's Throat: Opera, Homosexuality, and the Mystery of Desire* (a National Book Critics Circle Award finalist); *Jackie Under My Skin: Interpreting an Icon; Cleavage: Essays on Sex, Stars, and Aesthetics;* and *Andy Warhol. He has received a Whiting Writer's Award, and is currently a Professor of English at the City University of New York's Graduate Center.*

BOA EDITIONS, LTD.: AMERICAN POETS CONTINUUM SERIES

◈ COLOPHON ◈

Model Homes by Wayne Koestenbaum
was set in Bembo with Abobe Woodtype Ornaments
by Richard Foerster, York Beach, Maine.
The cover design is by Lisa Mauro.
The cover art, "House" (2002) by Jennifer Bartlett,
is courtesy of the artist.
Manufacturing was by United Graphics, Inc.,
Mattoon, Illinois.

◈

The publication of this book was made possible in part by the special
support of the following individuals:

Dr. & Mrs. Gary H. Conners
Dr. Henry & Beverly French
Judy & Dane Gordon
Kip & Deb Hale
Peter & Robin Hursh
Robert & Willy Hursh
Melissa Fondakowski
Archie & Pat Kutz
Glenn Ligon
Rosemary & Lew Lloyd
Boo Poulin
Deborah Ronnen
Allen & Suzy Spencer
Thomas R. Ward
Pat & Michael Wilder
Glenn & Helen William

◈